The Magic of
Salt Dough

With a seasonal flavour

BRIGITTE CASAGRANDA

SEARCH PRESS

To Marie, Sophie and Baptiste

First published in Great Britain 1997 by
SEARCH PRESS LIMITED
Wellwood, North Farm Road, Tunbridge Wells, Kent TN2 3DR

Originally published in France 1996 by
LAROUSSE-BORDAS
Original title: *Fetes et saisons* by Brigitte Casagranda
Copyright © Larousse-Bordas 1996

English translation © Search Press Limited 1997

Graphic design: Monique Wender
Editorial Director: Catherine Franck-Dandres
Editor: Ewa Lochet
English translation by G de la Bedoyère

All the subjects in this book are the creation of Brigitte Casagranda and may
not in any circumstance be reproduced for exhibition or sale.

ISBN 0 85532 830 4

The publishers advise caution in the use of
varnishes and white spirit by children.

Printed in Italy by G. Canale & C.S.p.A. Torino

Contents

Contents

Contents

Winter

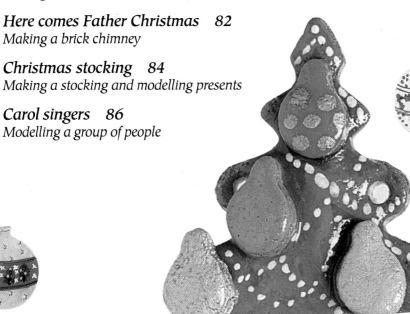

Basic techniques

Making natural dough

You will need:
> *Mixing bowl*
> *Measuring cup*
> *Wooden spoon*
> *Fine salt*
> *Flour*
> *Water*

Make the dough on a kitchen table or a waterproof surface. Ensure you have a damp sponge or cloth handy to keep the surface clean. It is advisable to wear an apron and to roll up your sleeves when working.

Dust the work surface with flour. Empty one cup of fine salt and two of flour into the mixing bowl and mix together with a

wooden spoon. Make a well in the mixture and add a cup of cold water. Mix all the ingredients in the bowl to form a dough. Transfer the dough on to the floured surface and knead it until it is malleable and smooth. If you find it

is too crumbly, add a little more water; if it is too sticky, add a little more flour. When it is smooth, free of air bubbles and easy to work, make a smooth ball ready for modelling. Soak or wash your equipment and clean the work top with a damp sponge.

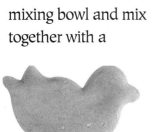

Colouring the dough

To colour the dough, use the same tools and ingredients as for natural dough. You will also need powdered spices, for example:

Cinnamon
Nutmeg
Curry
Cumin
Paprika
Ginger
Sweet Spanish
  pimento
White or black
  pepper
Chilli
Pure unsweetened
  cocoa

You can also use instant coffee granules, or half a cup of cold tea or coffee.

Empty a cup of flour into the bowl. The spices will not dissolve in water, so you should mix one level tablespoonful of your chosen spice with the flour. Add half a cup of salt and mix well. Pour half a cup of water into the bowl and mix all the ingredients with a wooden spoon and work as you would for natural dough.

After mixing up dough, cover it with polythene so that it does not dry out and let it 'rest' for thirty minutes. If you have coloured your dough, it will gradually darken as the spices begin to colour the salt and flour.

7

Modelling tools

Dough should not be kept for longer than twenty-four hours. After this time, it will not keep its shape if modelled.

There are lots of things you can use to help you model and decorate the salt dough. The following items are all used in this book:

Paint brush
Rolling pin
Biscuit cutters
Knife
Garlic press
Tea strainer or sieve
Pastry-wheel
Knitting needle
Drinking straw
Pliers
Wire

Cloves
Coriander seeds
Juniper berries
Fir cones
Moss
Small pieces of bark
Sticks
Silver foil / baking
  tray

Other items can be used to cut, shape or mould the dough. Biscuit cutters, like the ones shown above, are ideal, or you could cut out your own design using a sharp knife.

A few tips

Baking

The baking of models is a very important stage as it hardens and dries the dough.

Models should be placed on silver foil or on a baking tray, and initially baked on a gentle heat (100°C or 210°F) to dry the surface. After the required time, the silver foil or baking tray is removed and the model is placed in the middle of the oven, directly on the shelf. The baking then continues at a higher temperature (125°C or 260°F) until the model is completely dry.

Coloured salt dough should never be baked at more than 100°C (210°F), as the colours will fade.

Painting

A number of painting media are suitable for salt dough, in particular, non-waterproof ink, watercolour, gouache or acrylics. Acrylic paints include gold and a range of pearlescent colours.

Before painting, dust your model with a big, dry paint brush.

If the paint cracks after you have varnished it, try diluting it with a little water.

Varnishing

There are a variety of varnishes which can be used on the painted models: acrylic varnishes remain transparent and do not turn yellow; matt, gloss or satin-textured varnishes brighten the colours and protect the models from damp and dust. Clear wood varnish is especially effective on models which use coloured salt dough.

Varnish will protect a model, extend its life and enhance the colours. Usually two or three coats are needed.

Modelling a figure

Modelling

Take a small piece of dough and shape it into a smooth, slightly oval ball for the head. Put it on silver foil. Pinch one end of the oval ball to make the neck.

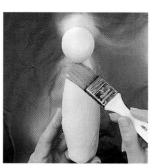

Make a roll of dough for the body and attach it to the neck by brushing with a little water.

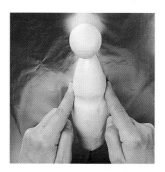

Pinch gently to make the waist.

If you are making a female figure, add a piece of dough to make the chest. Cover the body with a skirt and a jacket or shawl.

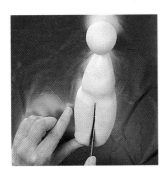

If you are making a male figure, slit the lower half of the body into two equal parts to create the trousers.

To make the shoes, shape small balls of dough. Mark each heel with a little notch.

To make the hair, use a garlic crusher, tea-strainer or sieve.

Add stripes to the trousers with a craft knife. Bend the legs and add crease marks with the side of a needle.

Making a hook

If you want to hang your figures up when finished, cut a length of wire, bend it like a hair-pin and slide it into the shoulders before baking. For other models or plaques you can make holes in the dough before baking. When painted and varnished you can thread a velvet ribbon, or length of raffia through the holes and use this to hang your model on the wall.

Make two rolls of dough for the arms. They must be angled away from the body. Do not shape them until the figure is completely clothed.

Once the arms have been finally positioned, make the hands. Take two little balls of dough, flatten them slightly and then score with a knife to suggest the fingers. Use a needle to place the hands in the sleeves or at the end of the arms.

Spring

Baskets of fruit

Modelling

Flatten a ball of dough to make the basket. Twist two lengths of dough together to form the handle, brush with water and secure to each side of the basket.

Create the wicker work using two forks.

Cut out some leaves and vein them with a knife. Roll small balls for the cherries and use dry twigs as their stalks. Attach the cherries and leaves with a wet brush.

Use a knife to score a different design on a second basket. This time, make some strawberries, and prick them lightly with a needle to give them their texture.

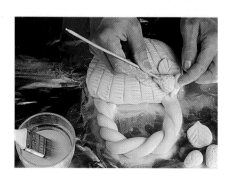

Baking

Bake at 100°C (210°F) for an hour. Remove the silver foil and continue baking for a further hour at 125°C (260°F).

Painting

Paint the model with acrylics. When dry, apply two or three coats of matt varnish.

Easter bunny

Modelling

Shape a ball for the head and a roll for the body. Slit the body a third of the way up,

then separate the two sections to make the legs. Roll two oval balls for the shoes.

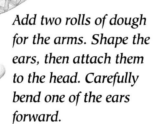

Add two rolls of dough for the arms. Shape the ears, then attach them to the head. Carefully bend one of the ears forward.

Model the two Easter eggs. Cut out thin strips of dough and wrap these round the eggs to form ribbons. Make and attach bows to the top of each egg.

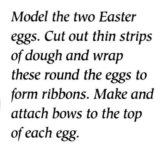

Attach one egg to the leg and the other to the stomach. The arms and hands should be positioned so that they rest on both eggs to keep them in place.

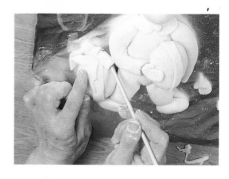

16

Baking

Bake for one hour at 100°C (210°F), then remove the silver foil and continue baking in the middle of the oven for a further one and a half hours at 125°C (260°F).

Painting

Use metallic acrylic paint for the egg-ribbons, and either acrylic or gouache for the rest of the model. When the paint is dry, apply two or three coats of gloss acrylic varnish.

Chicks in a nest

Modelling

Model the basket and create the wickerwork with a fork.

Roll a round ball for each chick's head, and an oval one for each body. Pinch the dough to make the tails.

Cut out the wings. Brush the dough with water and fix one wing to each body.

Place the chicks in position and support them with grass made with a garlic crusher. Add Easter eggs between the chicks.

Do not forget to insert wire hooks if you want to hang the model on the wall.

Baking

Bake for one hour at 100°C (210°F). Remove the silver foil, and bake for a further hour at 125°C (260°F) in the middle of the oven.

Painting

Use brown and orange inks diluted with water to paint the basket, and use green and yellow inks for the grass. Use acrylic paint for the chicks and the eggs – choose pastel colours such as yellow, pink, blue and mauve. When dry, apply gloss acrylic varnish.

Milkmaid

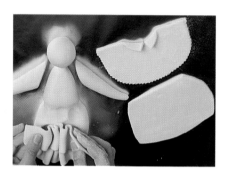

Modelling

Make the basic body shape. Cut out the pieces for the dress. Gently push the dough together to form pleats and attach to the body.

Use a garlic crusher to make the hair and attach to the head by brushing with a little water.

Cut a rectangle of dough for the bonnet, and notch the edges with a pastry-wheel. Fold the dough to form lots of pleats and then place the bonnet on the head.

Add the clogs, the milk-pot and the cat, making sure that they are all well supported. Brush the dough with water to ensure that everything will remain attached during baking.

Baking

Bake for one hour at 100°C (210°F). Remove the silver foil and bake for a further two and a half hours at 125°C (260°F).

Painting

Use inks for the hair and acrylic paints for the rest of the model. When dry, apply matt varnish.

Cabbage patch

Modelling

Cut out the bonnet and attach half of the hair.

Dampen the head and then put the bonnet in place. Attach the rest of the hair, using a needle to shape each strand.

Make the cabbages from small balls of dough and then arrange leaves around each of them as shown.

Brush the dough with water and then attach the cabbages to the dress.

Ensure that all parts of the model are properly attached before baking.

Baking

Bake for one hour at 100°C (210°F). Remove the silver foil and then bake for a further two hours at 125°C (260°F).

Painting

Before painting, use a clean, dry paint brush to dust down your model and remove any flour. Use water-colour paints for the face and acrylics for the body. Apply two coats of gloss acrylic varnish.

23

Feeding the cows

Modelling

Make a base for your model. Place it on silver foil and flatten it with your palm. Add the fence.

Make the basic shape of the little boy. Brush him with water then sit him on the fence and attach him firmly.

Add the grass. Model the cows and support their horns and ears with pieces of silver foil which you can remove halfway through baking. Cut out the birds and attach to the fence.

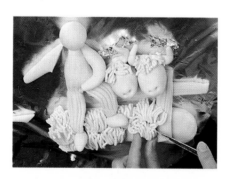

Model the little boy's hands. Score the fingers with a sharp knife and then attach to the arms. Cut out the jacket and put it in position.

Cut round a template to make the flowers and use a garlic crusher to make the grass. Arrange the grass and flowers on the model using the tip of a sharp knife. Insert two wire hooks, one behind the boy's shoulder, the other behind one of the cows.

Baking

Bake for one hour at 100°C (210°F). Remove all the silver foil and then bake for a further hour at 125°C (260°F).

Painting

Paint the small boy, his straw hat, the grass and the flowers with inks. Paint the cows and birds with acrylics. When dry, apply two coats of gloss acrylic varnish.

Dozing miller

Modelling

Flatten a base to a thickness of 1.5cm (¹/₂in). Cut out the windmill and place it on the base. Using a sharp knife, draw on the door, window and brickwork. Use small flattened balls to make the roof tiles.

Brush the dough with water before joining pieces together. Make sure all the parts of the model are firmly attached before baking.

Model the sails on a separate piece of silver foil. Bake in the oven for fifteen–twenty minutes at 100°C (210°F). When cool, brush the sails with water and attach to the roof.

Make the grass using a garlic crusher. Now model the little miller, the sacks of flour and the leaves and flowers.

Baking

Bake the model at 100°C (210°F) for one hour. Remove the silver foil and bake for a further two hours at 125°C (260°F).

Painting

Use inks to paint this model. The more you dilute the inks, the softer and more transparent they become. You can use this method to make different tones of the same colour for the roof of the windmill and the sails. When dry, apply two coats of matt varnish.

27

Little green mouse

Modelling

Use your palm to flatten a base to a thickness of 1cm (³/₈in). Model the little girl and attach her to the base. Add the legs, shoes, head, clothes and the grass.

Arrange the arms behind the girl's back, then add the hair. Bake for thirty minutes.

Whilst the model is baking, make the hat, the ribbon and the bow. Cut round a template to make the flowers and the leaves. Attach all these pieces to the model once it has cooled.

Put the model back in the oven for fifteen minutes and whilst this is baking, make the mouse. Bake the mouse separately for ten minutes.

Baking

Put the part-completed model in the oven for thirty minutes at 100°C (210°F). Attach the hat, ribbon, bow, flowers and leaves and replace in the oven for fifteen minutes. Model the mouse and bake this separately for ten minutes at 100°C (210°F). Add the hands, then dampen the mouse and position it head down. Check that all the parts are properly attached before baking the completed model for one hour at 100°C (210°F). Remove the silver foil and bake for a further hour at 125°C (260°F).

Painting

Paint the model with inks. When dry, apply matt acrylic varnish.

Gathering rosebuds

Modelling

*Make a base and attach
a fence to it. Now model
the girl. Cut out the
apron from a rectangle
of dough and gently
pinch into position.*

*Cut out the leaves and
model the flowers as
shown. Position
them on the base
and at the foot of the
fence.*

*Carefully pinch out the
apron so that it will
support the flowers.*

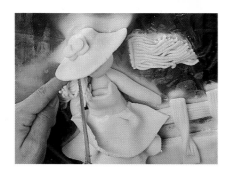

*Model a wide-brimmed
hat, and position a bow
at the front. Place the
hat on the girl's head.
Make the hair using a
garlic crusher, and use
the tip of a knife to
attach it underneath the
hat. Brush the apron
with water and then
attach roses to it. Insert
wire hooks in the
shoulders so you can
hang the model on the
wall when finished.*

30

Baking

Bake for one hour at 100°C (210°F). Remove the silver foil. Bake for a further hour at 125°C (260°F).

Painting

Paint the model with inks. When dry, apply three coats of gloss acrylic varnish.

Summer

Wheelbarrow

Modelling

Model the pieces for the wheelbarrow as shown, then bake for thirty–forty minutes at 100°C (210°F). Leave to cool.

Insert one end of a wooden toothpick into the wheel and attach to the back of the body of the wheelbarrow with a thick dough paste, made by adding water to the usual mixture. Model and instal the little boy in the wheelbarrow, then attach the other little boy. Insert two wire hooks.

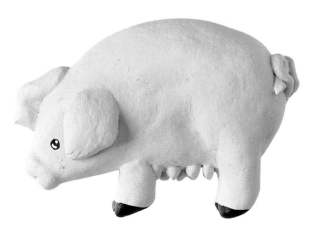

Baking

Bake the completed model for one hour at 100°C (210°F). Remove the silver foil making sure the wheel stays attached. Bake for a further hour at 125°C (260°F).

Painting

Paint the wheelbarrow with heavily diluted acrylics then apply three coats of matt acrylic varnish. When completely dry, use wood glue to stick on dried grasses (clover and wild clematis have been used here). Finally, thread two lengths of raffia through the wire hooks and knot them together.

Harvesting wheat

Modelling

Model the head and the body. Pinch in the waist and attach the clogs. Flatten out a piece of dough then use a decorative button to print a regular design. Cut out a rectangle from the patterned dough to make the skirt.

Brush the body with water then attach the skirt. Gently form the pleats then swirl up the bottom of the skirt to suggest movement. Now add the bodice. Bake the model at 100°C (210°F) for one hour.

  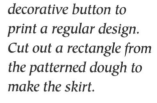

Whilst the model is baking, make the wheat sheaf as shown. When complete, bake for ten minutes. Make the knotted rope for the wheat sheaf, the arms, the hands and the bonnet.

Attach the arms, then the wheat sheaf (which will have slightly hard-ened), then the hands, bonnet and rope, and finally the hair. Insert a wire hook in each shoulder.

Baking

Bake the part-completed model for one hour at 100°C (210°F) and bake the wheat sheaf for ten minutes. Remove the silver foil, attach all the pieces and bake in the centre of the oven for a further two and a half hours at 125°C (260°F).

Painting

Paint the wheat sheaf and clogs with inks and use well-diluted acrylic paints for the dress and bonnet. When dry, apply three coats of varnish to protect the model.

Leapfrog

Modelling

Flatten a piece of dough with your palm to a thickness of about 1.5cm (¹/₂in). Model the first little boy, then make the wheat using a garlic crusher. Attach both to the base.

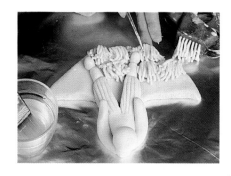

Bake the model for fifteen minutes at 100°C (210°F). Meanwhile, model the wheat sheaves and the second boy. Make his head and bake separately for ten minutes.

Insert a toothpick or twig into the second boy's body and attach him to the first boy. Brush the base with water and attach the wheat sheaves.

Insert two wire hooks then put the model back in the oven and bake for twenty minutes at 100°C (210°F). Remove from the oven and attach the second boy's head (which will have already hardened). Make and then attach the two caps.

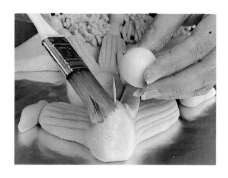

Painting

Paint the corn with inks and the little boys with acrylics. When dry, apply three coats of gloss acrylic varnish.

Baking

Bake the completed model for one hour at 100°C (210°F). Remove the silver foil and bake for a further one and a half hours at 125°C (260°F).

Field mice

Modelling

Model the ears of maize – these will act as supports for the mice. Roll tiny balls of dough to make the grains and stick them in place.

Cut out the leaves. Use a sharp knife to add texture then assemble over the grains of maize.

Model the mice in a similar way to figures. First make the head, then the ears, arms, feet, tail, nose and finally the little paws.

Brush the ears of maize with water. Attach the stalks and then arrange the mice. Make sure the mice are attached at as many points as possible to keep them secure.

Remember to insert wire hooks into the stalks before baking.

Baking

This thick model should bake for one hour at 100°C (210°F). Remove the silver foil, then bake for a further two hours at 125°C (260°F).

Painting

Paint the maize with inks, and use acrylics for the mice. Apply three coats of gloss acrylic varnish. When dry, thread pieces of raffia through the wire hooks and tie in a big bow.

Little Miss Prim

Modelling

Flatten some dough with a rolling pin, then cut out strips 0.5cm (¹/₄in) wide. Arrange these to form a trellis. Cut out the arch and attach it to the trellis frame.

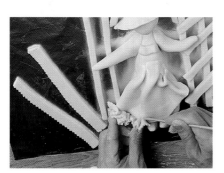

Model the girl's head and body. Cut out the dress and notch the hem with a pastry-wheel. Attach the dress and arrange it into pleats as shown.

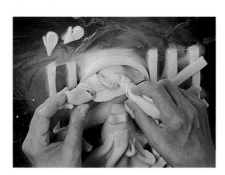

Bake the the girl and the trellis for two hours at 100°C (210°F). Meanwhile, make the bouquet – use a garlic crusher for the stalks, and then add the flowers and leaves. Bake for ten minutes. Now make more leaves and flowers for the trellis. Model the arms, the hands and the hat. Gently twist a length of dough to form the ribbon to go around the hat.

Brush the model with water then attach the arms, bouquet, hands, hat and the ribbon. Position the leaves and the flowers on the trellis. Insert two wire hooks.

Baking

Bake the part-completed model for two hours at 100°C. (210°F), and bake the bouquet for half and hour. Turn the model over on to a teatowel. Gently unpeel the silver foil. Attach all the pieces and place the model in the centre of the oven. Bake for a further hour at 125°C (260°F).

Painting

Use pearlescent acrylics for the dress and the ribbon on the hat, and normal acrylics for the rest of the model. Apply three coats of gloss acrylic varnish. It is worth taking time over the painting of clothing as such detail can make all the difference to the finished model.

Milking time

Modelling

Flatten a piece of dough with your palm to make a base for the model. Make the cow and the bell as shown.

Model the little boy, the stool, the milkcan and the bucket. Use a garlic crusher to make the grass. Position the little boy on the stool.

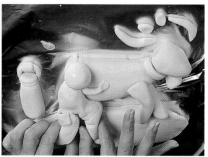

Make sure that all the pieces are well-attached. Add more grass to strengthen the model.

To make the cat, roll a dough ball for the head and attach two pointed ears. Shape a roll for the body and put the tail in position.

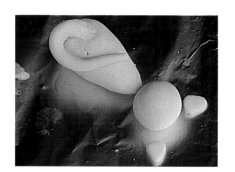

Baking

Bake the model for one hour at 100°C (210°F). Remove the silver foil and bake for a further two hours at 125°C (260°F).

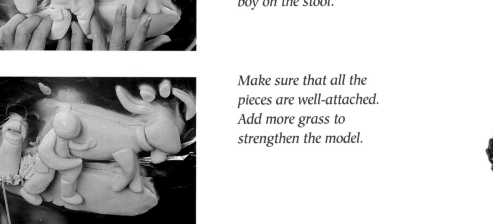

Painting

Paint the grass with heavily-diluted yellow and green inks. Paint the rest of the model in acrylics, then apply three coats of gloss acrylic varnish.

Siesta

Modelling

Use your palm to flatten a base to a thickness of 1.5cm ($^{1}/_{2}$in). Use a garlic crusher to make grass, and place this around the pond. Add a few stooks of corn and model the sleeping boy.

Baking

Bake the model for one hour at 100°C (210°F). Remove the silver foil and bake for a further hour at 125°C (260°F).

Painting

Use inks to paint the entire model. When dry, apply three coats of gloss acrylic varnish.

Cut out the water-lily leaves and the flowers and place them on the pond along with a duck. Add leaves to the bank of the pond.

Shepherdess

Modelling

Flatten out a base 1.5cm (¹/₂in) thick. Model the shepherdess, beginning with her head and body, then her chest, feet and apron. Add the bonnet and then make the plaits for the hair using three thin ropes of dough. Position the hair under the bonnet.

Shape the arms and then cut out a semicircle of dough with a pastry-wheel to make the shawl. Use a knife to make the fringe, then cut the shawl in half. Brush the arms and shoulders with water and drape the two halves of the shawl over both shoulders. Add the hands and lightly mark in the wrists using a needle. Remember to leave the hands open so that they can hold the dried grass. Place the model in the oven and bake for one hour at 100°C (210°F).

Meanwhile, model the goats and sheep, using dough squeezed through a strainer to make their fleeces. Bake them for ten minutes.

Add grass, which you can make using a garlic crusher. Brush the goats and sheep with water and attach to the grass.

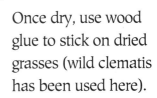

Baking

Bake the part-completed model for one hour at 100°C (210°F) and bake the goats and sheep for ten minutes. Remove the silver foil, attach all the pieces and bake for a further two hours at 125°C (260°F).

Painting

Paint the shepherdess in acrylics and use watercolour for the face. Leave the dough its natural colour for the sheep and goats. Apply three coats of gloss varnish.

To check that the model is dry, tap the back. It should sound hollow – if it doesn't, continue baking and re-check every fifteen minutes.

Once dry, use wood glue to stick on dried grasses (wild clematis has been used here).

Bird mobile

Modelling

This mobile is very easy to make. Flatten the dough to a thickness of 0.5cm (¼in). Make a template for the birds, place it on the dough and cut round it. Make a hole through each bird so you can eventually thread through raffia and hang them up.

There are lots of birds to choose from, but the crossbill, red Bengali, bernacle goose, wren, magpie, wagtail and sheldrake all make good models as they are so colourful.

Baking

Bake the birds for one hour at 100°C (210°F), then for a further thirty minutes at 125°C (260°F).

Painting

Paint the birds with gouache and acrylics, then apply gloss varnish. When dry, thread raffia through the holes and attach the birds to a bamboo cane.

Modelling

Flatten the dough to a thickness of 0.5cm (¼in). Put a template for the outer plaque shape on the dough and cut round it. Place on silver foil then position a smaller template in the middle and cut out the centre hole. Decorate with miniature models and stick in place by brushing with water. Make two holes at the top of each decoration for the raffia to be threaded through.

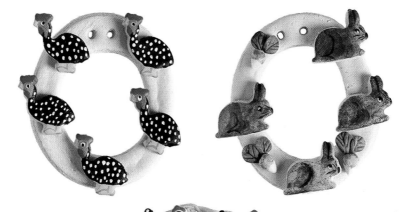

Baking

Bake for one hour at 100°C (210°F), then for thirty minutes at 125°C (260°F).

Autumn

Apple tree

Modelling

Make up some coloured dough using cocoa. Flatten the dough to make the tree trunk and branches. Mark the bark in with a knife.

Mix up two coloured doughs. Break the dough into small pieces and then roll together to form a marbled dough. Cut out lots of leaves from the marbled dough and mark in the veins with a knife. Brush with a little water and arrange them in clusters, with the leaves overlapping. Model the apples from dough coloured with sweet Spanish pimento. Push cloves into the apples to make the stalks. Fix a wire hook to the back of the tree.

Baking

Bake the apple tree for one hour at 100°C (210°F). Remove the silver foil and bake for a further thirty minutes at the same temperature. Leave to cool, then apply two or three coats of clear wood varnish (you can use either matt, gloss or satin finish).

54

Wreaths

Coloured wreath

Make two ropes from dough coloured with cumin. Brush with water, twist them together and shape to form a circle. Make the leaves from dough coloured with black pepper and the apples from dough coloured with cocoa. Make some of the flowers from natural, uncoloured dough and others from dough coloured with paprika. Press in cloves and juniper berries to make the flower heads. Bake for one hour at 100°C (210°F), removing the silver foil at the halfway stage.

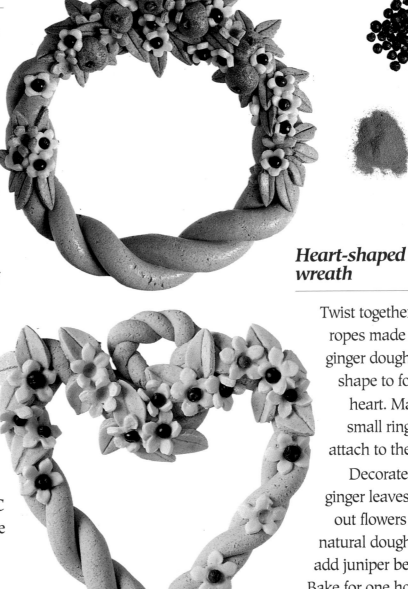

Heart-shaped wreath

Twist together two ropes made from ginger dough and shape to form a heart. Make a small ring and attach to the top. Decorate with ginger leaves. Cut out flowers from natural dough and add juniper berries. Bake for one hour at 100°C (210°F), removing the silver foil at the halfway stage.

Twists

Twist together two ropes of dough and then decorate with leaves, fruit or flowers.

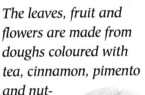

The leaves, fruit and flowers are made from doughs coloured with tea, cinnamon, pimento and nut- meg.

Add juniper berries, cloves or aniseed. Decorate the apple segment with real pips and a real stalk.

Bake for two hours at 100°C (210°F), re- moving the silver foil after an hour.

Apply three coats of clear wood varnish, allowing plenty of time to dry between each coat.

Fruit wreath

Twist two ropes of dough together. Brush with water and shape to form a circle. Use ginger dough to make the leaves. Arrange them around the wreath. Add the ap- ples and the pears (made from curry dough). Bake for one hour at 100°C (210°F). Remove the silver foil after half an hour.

Scarecrow

Modelling

Model the head from dough coloured with tea. Push it on to the end of a stick.

Cut out the trousers and pockets from curry dough. Make a button from natural dough. Put sticks in place for the arms.

Cut out the jacket and one pocket from black pepper dough. Shape the lapels. Use a needle to pinch in the coat at the waist.

Add the sleeves and position the hat. Use lichen for the hands, juniper berries for the eyes and a coriander seed for the nose.

Just like a real scarecrow, this model is made on a base of sticks which are arranged to form a cross.

Remember to insert wire hooks into each shoulder so you can hang your model on the wall.

Baking

Bake for thirty minutes at 100°C (210°F). Remove the silver foil and bake for a further hour at the same temperature.

Painting

Paint on a smile using gouache. When dry, apply clear wood varnish. Stick moss under the hat to make the hair and stuff moss into the trouser-bottoms to make the feet. Put a piece of string around his waist for a belt, and use another piece around the neck.

59

Woodcutter

Modelling

Roll a slightly oval ball for the head and pinch the base to make the neck. Place this on silver foil. Use a roll of dough for the body, brush it with water and attach to the head. Pinch the dough to

mark the waist. Cut the lower half of the body into two equal parts to create the legs. To make corduroy trousers, use a knife to add stripes. Bend one of the legs and mark in the trouser creases with a needle.

Use two rolls of dough to make the arms. They must be angled away from the body until the figure is completely clothed. To make the coat, flatten the dough using a floured rolling-pin. Cut out the jacket

in two parts and put in place. Add buttons and pockets if you wish. For the clogs, roll two little balls of dough. Mark in the heels with a knife, then pinch the ends to make the toes.

Position the arms around a bundle of sticks tied with string. Flatten two little balls to make the hands. Score in the fingers then use a needle to attach the hands inside the

sleeves. Model and position the hat. Make the hair by feeding dough through a garlic crusher or a strainer. Alternatively, flatten a piece of dough and cut it into thin strips.

Baking

Bake for one hour at 100°C (210°F). Remove the silver foil and bake for a further two hours at 125°C until the model is completely dry.

Painting

Paint the model with inks which you can dilute. When dry, apply two coats of gloss acrylic varnish.

Modelling

Roll a ball for the head and pinch the base to form the neck. Make a roll for the body and attach it to the neck. Pinch the dough to mark the waist. Add the *chest, then build out the skirt by pressing your index finger into the dough. Position the arms. Shape and position the clogs and make the hands.*

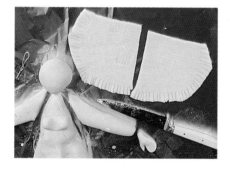

Flatten some dough and cut out a semi-circle for the shawl. Use a decorative button to print a design on the shawl.

Notch the curved edge with a pastry-wheel or use a knife to make the fringe. Cut in half.

Fix each half of the shawl on to the figure, and position the arms.

Add the bundle of sticks and position the hands. Cut out thin strips of dough for the hair. To make the bun at the back, feed dough through a garlic crusher. Insert two wire hooks into the back of the shoulders.

Baking

Bake for one hour at 100°C (210°F). Remove the silver foil and bake for a further two hours at 125°C (260°F) until completely dry.

Painting

Paint the model with heavily diluted inks, so as to leave the texture of the dough showing through. When dry, apply two coats of gloss acrylic varnish.

Chestnuts

Modelling

Flatten dough coloured with curry. Cut out five leaves and arrange them on silver foil. Add the stalks.

Score in the veins on the leaves. Roll three small balls of dough coloured with cinnamon.

Wrap each ball in a thin layer of nutmeg dough, leaving just a little of the cinnamon dough showing at the top. Make sure your hands are clean and dry before reshaping into smooth balls. Brush the leaves with a little water, then position the chestnuts in a cluster.

Baking

Bake for half an hour at 100°C (210°F). Remove the silver foil and bake for a further thirty minutes at the same temperature. Apply three coats of clear wood varnish.

Sleepy fox

Baking

Bake for one hour at 100°C (210°F). Remove the silver foil and bake for a further thirty minutes at 125°C (260°F).

Painting

Paint the model using inks. When dry, apply gloss acrylic varnish.

Modelling

Roll a ball for the head and pinch the end to form a point. Put it on silver foil. Model a larger, slightly oval ball for the body. Attach it to the head and bend it into a crescent shape. Use a small ball of dough to make the nose.

Make a crescent of dough for the tail. Brush with a little water and attach it to the body. Add the ears. Finally, surround the fox with leaves and toadstools.

Frog

Modelling

This model uses dough coloured with ground black pepper. Be careful when mixing it as it can make your eyes and nose sting.

Use a thick roll of dough to make the head and body. Make a little cushion of silver foil to support the head during modelling and baking.

Roll two small balls for the eyes and press a juniper berry into each. Use a needle to draw in the mouth and nostrils. Model the legs, making

sure that the front ones are shorter than the back ones. Use a needle and tiny balls of dough to make the webbed feet.

Baking

Bake for forty minutes at 100°C (210°F). Remove the silver foil and bake for a further thirty minutes at the same temperature. Apply three coats of matt acrylic varnish.

Toadstools

Modelling

Mix up some natural dough and some dough coloured with curry, tea and sweet Spanish pimento to make the toadstools.

Shape the toadstools and score their under-sides with a knife.

Chocolate bear cub

Modelling

This model is made with dough coloured with pure, unsweetened cocoa. Use a ball for the head, and two small flattened balls for the ears. Use a thick roll for the body and mark in the navel with a needle.

Slit the lower half of the body into two equal parts to make the legs. Make the boots and the arms and use a small ball of dough for the muzzle.

Brush all the pieces with water and assemble the cub. Use juniper berries for the eyes and the nose.

Baking

Bake for thirty minutes at 100°C (210°F). Remove the silver foil and bake for a further thirty minutes at the same temperature. Leave to cool, then apply two coats of clear wood varnish.

Red squirrel

Modelling

Roll a small oval ball for the head, and a bigger one for the body. Brush the head with water and attach to the body. Feed a length of dough through a garlic press, then curl it round at the top to make the tail. Attach it to the body.

Add the paws, then the nut and finally the ears. Do not forget to add wire hooks in both shoulders.

Baking

Bake for one hour at 100°C (210°F). Remove the silver foil and bake for a further thirty minutes at 125°C (260°F).

Painting

Paint the model with inks. When dry, apply three coats of acrylic gloss varnish.

Halloween

Modelling

Use a big ball for the head, a thick roll for the body, two short rolls for the legs and two longer ones for the arms. Add two small oval balls for the clogs. Mark in the heels with a knife and pinch the ends to make the toes.

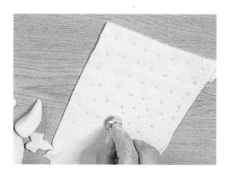

To make the jacket, flatten the dough then stamp a design on to it using a decorative button. Cut out a rectangle, drape it over the body, then push the top together to form pleats. Cut out leaves and use these to make the collar.

Mark in the nose, eyes, eyebrows and mouth using a modelling tool. Use this tool to make the mouth bigger and to emphasise the chin. Add the horns.

Baking

Bake for one hour at 100°C (210°F), then for a further hour at 125°C (260°F).

Painting

Paint the jacket with inks, which will allow the design to show through. Paint the clogs with inks and the rest of the model with acrylics. Apply two coats of acrylic varnish.

Giraffes and zebras

Modelling

Flatten some coloured dough, then arrange little balls of natural dough on top. Use a rolling-pin to press them into the coloured dough and roll to a thickness of 0.5cm ($^1/_4$in). Cut out the giraffes with a biscuit cutter.

To make zebras, use the same technique, but this time arrange strips of coloured dough on natural dough.

Make sure the strips are spaced evenly before flattening them with a rolling-pin.

Cut out the zebras with a biscuit cutter. Use a drinking straw to make holes in each model so you can attach them to one another.

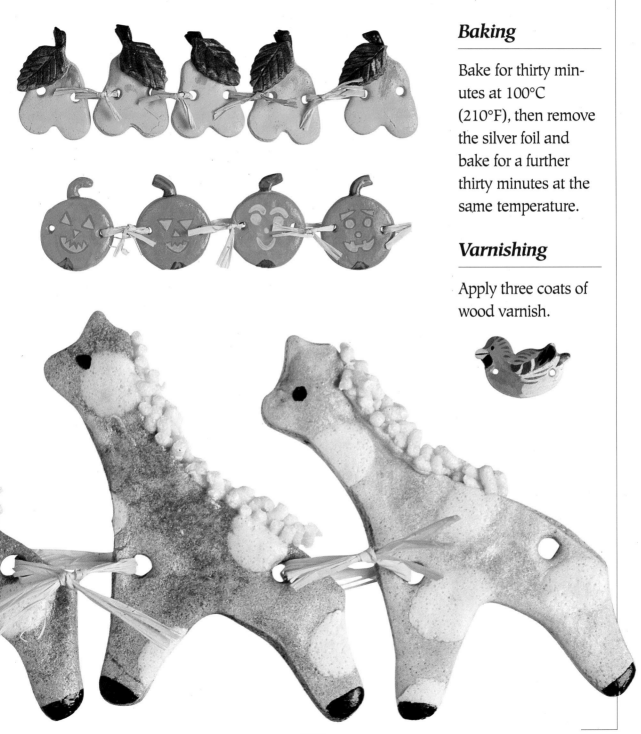

Baking

Bake for thirty minutes at 100°C (210°F), then remove the silver foil and bake for a further thirty minutes at the same temperature.

Varnishing

Apply three coats of wood varnish.

Winter

Winter window

Modelling

Cut out a rectangle, then remove a smaller rectangle from its centre. Smooth the inside top corners with your finger and cut the outside corners to form points. Place two strips of dough inside the window to form a cross.

Make some berries and cut out the leaves with a knife. Arrange them above the window. Mark in the stone bricks with a knife. Make two strips of dough. Brush them with water and add to make the roof. Bake the model for fifteen minutes at 100°C (210°F).

Remove from the oven. Brush the top of the roof with water and add snow here and on the window. To make the little girl, roll a ball for the head, another for the body and use two strips for the arms. Flatten two little balls of dough for the hands and use a garlic crusher to make the hair. Position her at the window. Insert two wire hooks.

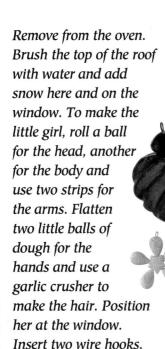

Baking

Bake the finished model for thirty minutes at 100°C (210°F). Remove the silver foil and bake for a further hour at 125°C (260°F).

Painting

Paint the window with acrylics. If you use white acrylic for the snow, make sure you apply acrylic varnish to prevent the paint from cracking.

Away in a manger

Modelling

Squeeze the dough through a garlic crusher to make the manger. Make a hollow in the centre with your finger and brush with water.

To make the baby, use a round ball for the head and an oval one for the body. Use two rolls for the arms and two small balls for the hands.

Place the baby in the straw manger. To make the swaddling clothes, use bands of dough notched with a pastry-wheel or patterned with a drinking straw. Add a small strip of dough for the bonnet.

Baking

Bake for thirty minutes at 100°C (210°F). Remove the silver foil and bake for a further thirty minutes at 125°C (260°F).

Painting

Paint the model with water-colours or inks. Try to choose soft colours. When dry, apply three coats of matt or gloss clear wood varnish.

Modelling

Use a ball for each head and pinch in one end to form the neck. Add a roll for each body. Mark in the waists and then slightly flatten the lower half of each body with your finger.

To make the clothing, cut out two rectangles from a piece of flattened dough. Drape one over each body, then gently push the tops together to form pleats. Add the arms, hands and shoes. Model baby Jesus, brush with a little water and position in the fold of Mary's arm.

Feed dough through a garlic crusher to make Mary's hair, and through a tea strainer to make Joseph's. Cut out the stars and join them together to form an arch. Attach Mary to one end, and Joseph to the other.

Baking

Bake for one hour at 100°C (210°F). Remove the silver foil and bake for a further hour at 125°C (260°F).

Painting

Paint Mary with acrylics and Joseph with inks. Varnish.

Modelling

For each snowman, roll a ball for the body, then a smaller one for the head. Brush with water and then attach them to each other.

Cut out a long thin strip for the scarf. Add the fringe using a knife, and cut in half. Attach both pieces to the snowman. Slightly flatten two little balls to make the gloves and mark in the thumbs. Put in place. Model then attach the bobble hat and insert wire hooks in the hat.

Baking

Bake for thirty minutes at 100°C (210°F). Remove the silver foil and bake for a further thirty minutes at 125°C (260°F).

Painting

Paint the snowmen all over in white acrylic. Allow to dry and then paint the bobble hats, scarves and gloves in bright colours. Decorate with stripes and dots. Paint on the eyes, nose and mouth. When dry, apply three coats of gloss or matt acrylic varnish.

Little angels

Modelling

Flatten some dough to a thickness of 0.5cm (¹/₄in). Cut out the moons and shooting stars with biscuit cutters. Roll round balls for the angels' heads and oval ones for their bodies. Attach them to each other, then position on a shooting star or on a moon. Add little rolls for the arms. Cut out smaller stars and moons for decoration. Gently insert wire hooks into the angels' shoulders, making sure the angels keep their shape.

Baking

Bake for thirty minutes at 100°C (210°F). Remove the silver foil and bake for a further thirty minutes at 125°C (260°F).

Painting

Paint the models with gold and pearlescent acrylics. When dry, apply three coats of gloss acrylic varnish.

Modelling

Flatten a dough rectangle to a thickness of 2.5cm (1in) for the chimney. Draw in the bricks with a knife. Add a band of dough for the base and another for the chimney-top.

Make Father Christmas using a slightly oval ball for the body. Add a small round ball for his head and two rolls for his arms. Make two flattened balls for his gloves.

Make and attach the hat and pompom. Use a tea strainer to make the fur trim for the hat. Use a needle to gently raise the arms, and position a sack under one of them. Put the gloves into position using a needle. Cut out the beard and moustache and score with the tip of a sharp knife to distinguish them from the fur on the hat.

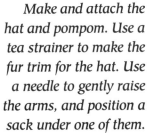

Add holly leaves and berries to the base of the chimney. Make sure that all the pieces are properly attached before inserting a wire hook into each shoulder.

Baking

Bake for one hour
at 100°C (210°F).
Remove the silver
foil and bake for
a further hour at
125°C (260°F).

Painting

Paint with acrylics or
gouache, then apply
three coats of glossy
or matt clear
wood varnish.

Modelling

Flatten the dough to a thickness of 1cm (³/₈in). Cut out the basic stocking shape then cut out the heel and smooth it with your finger.

Cut out the rim for the stocking. Notch it with a pastry wheel or cut out a zig-zag design.

Flatten out a piece of dough at the top of the stocking – you can use this as a base to arrange the toys on.

Add pompoms. Model little dolls, baubles and parcels. Brush the dough with a little water before attaching the presents. Insert two wire hooks at the back of the stocking.

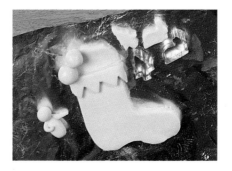

Baking

Bake the model for thirty minutes at 100°C (210°F). Remove the silver foil then bake for a further thirty minutes at 125°C (260°F).

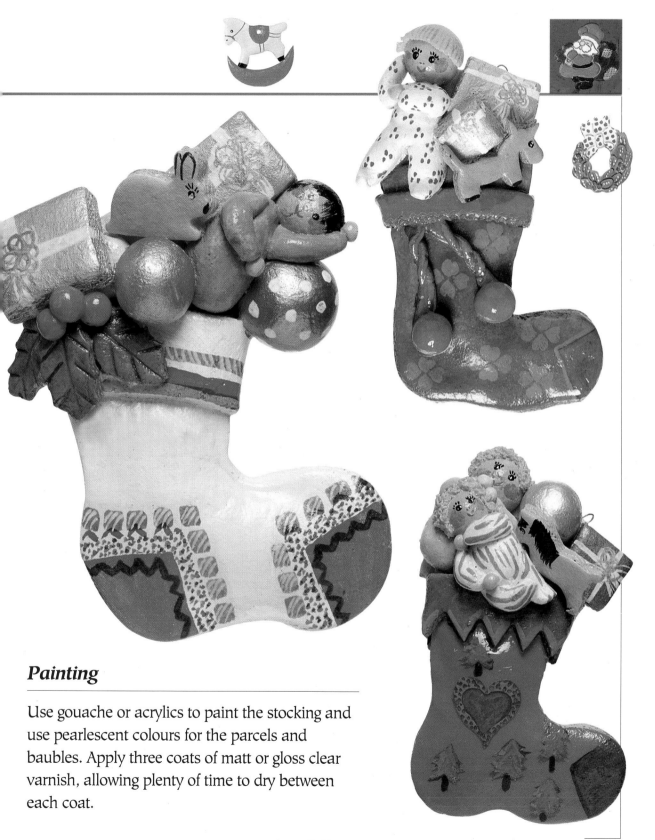

Painting

Use gouache or acrylics to paint the stocking and use pearlescent colours for the parcels and baubles. Apply three coats of matt or gloss clear varnish, allowing plenty of time to dry between each coat.

Carol singers

Modelling

This model takes a little while to make, but it is not difficult. The figures are joined together by their arms and legs to make the model strong. Do not forget to insert wire hooks so you can hang up the finished model.

Baking

Bake for one hour at 100°C (210°F). Remove the silver foil and bake for a further hour at 125°C (260°F). If the underside of the model is still soft after this time, continue baking for thirty more minutes at 125°C (260°F).

Painting

Paint the model with gouache or acrylics, then apply matt or gloss clear wood varnish.

87

Carnival clown

Modelling

Shape the body. Slit the lower half to create the legs. Add the arms and gently pinch and flatten the dough to make the shape of the suit.

Cut out two collars with a pastry-wheel. Arrange them into pleats then use a needle to place them, one on top of the other, around the neck.

Cut out tiny rectangles for the playing cards and join them by gently pressing together. Make the mask, using a needle to shape the eyebrows. Pinch the dough to make the nose, then shape it into a beak. Add two little balls for the cheeks and smooth over the dough. Make the eyes by piercing with a drinking straw.

Baking

Bake the model for one hour at 100°C (210°F). Remove the silver foil, then bake for a further two and a half hours at 125°C (260°F).

Painting

Paint the suit using heavily diluted red ink. Use acrylics for the collar, playing cards and mask. Apply two coats of gloss acrylic varnish.

Friendly tiger

Modelling

To model the tiger, make a ball for the head and a roll for the body, slit at the base to form legs. Roll two oval balls for the feet, brush with water and put in position. Make two strips for the arms and a thin rope for the tail which you can drape around the shoulder.

Cover the head in a thin strip of dough, leaving the face area free. Make two small balls for the ears, flatten them slightly then attach to the head. Add an ice-cream cone and attach the hands.

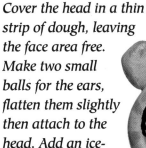

Baking

Bake for one hour at 100°C (210°F). Remove the silver foil then bake for a further two hours at 125°C (260°F).

Daisy

Modelling

Model the body and the head, then add the arms, hands and two small balls for the feet. Use a pastry-cutter or a knife to cut out the leaves and overlap them to make the skirt. Flatten oval pieces of dough to make the petals and arrange around the head.

Position the arms. Pinch some leaves around the neck to form a collar. Stick a leaf on each shoe, and add a little flower.

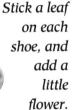

You can easily make a forget-me-not or a red poppy instead of a daisy by simply changing the shape and colour of the leaves and petals.

Baking

Bake for one hour at 100°C (210°F), then remove the silver foil. Bake for two hours at 125°C (260°F).

91

Young prince

Modelling

Make a roll for the body. Pinch it in at the waist. With your finger, flatten the dough beneath the waist to prepare a base for the skirt. Make a ball for the head, two balls for the shoes, two long rolls for the arms and two short ones for the legs.

Flatten the dough to a thickness of 0.5cm (¼in). Cut out a crown, then a rectangle for the skirt which you should gather in at the waist. Cut the waistcoat out in two sections. Position on the figure.

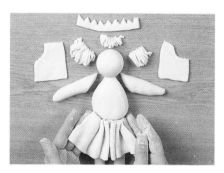

Make the hair in three sections and put into position using a needle. Place the crown on top.

Lightly brush the shoes with water and attach the bows. Model the playing cards. Add the hands and score in the fingers with a needle.

Baking

Bake the model for one hour at 100°C (210°F). Remove the silver foil and bake for a further two hours at 125°C (260°F).

Painting

Paint the model using acrylics. Use bronze for the sleeves; maroon for the skirt, legs and shoes; and gold for the bows and crown. When dry, apply two coats of gloss acrylic varnish.

Knight in shining armour

Modelling

Model a ball for the head. Brush with a little water and add a roll for the body. Pinch in at the waist. Slit the lower half of the body and divide to form the legs.

Make the armour by pinching and by using a needle. Pinch in the leg-guards and attach the shield. Cut out the shoulder-guards and the pieces for the helmet.

Position the helmet, then add the pattern to the helmet and the shoulder-guards. Brush with water and attach to the knight. Add the gauntlets.

Baking

Bake for one hour at 100°C (210°F), then remove the silver foil and bake for a further two hours at 125°C (260°F).

Painting

Paint the armour with silver acrylic. To add a splash of colour, paint the shield in red and white. Apply two coats of gloss acrylic varnish. When dry, paint a pipecleaner red. Cut it into three short pieces and use to make the plumage for the helmet.

Index